*

*

extended remark: poems from a moravian parking lot

*

for a fellow poet

---

extended remark: poems from a moravian parking lot

Michael Martin

Best,

Michael Martin

Front cover streetlight photo by Daniel Oines

Back cover photo of the author by Ann Gollin

extended remark: poems from a moravian parking lot
by Michael Martin

Published by Portals Press
New Orleans, Louisiana USA
www.portalspress.com

ISBN 978-0-916620-26-4

Acknowledgments

Much appreciation to the editors of the magazines (and blog) where the following poems first appeared:

Berkeley Poetry Review: "Work"
Russell Shorto Blog: "Village," "Little Walter
Returns From The Dead To Deliver A Mournful,
Seaside Elegy At Blues Harmonica Camp"
Booth Journal: "My Bobcat Skid-Steer Loader Is My Therapy"
Carolina Quarterly: "Three Seconds Of Bright Light," "Public
Service Announcement From Last Night's Dream"
Chattahoochee Review: "Thieves," "Cigarettes"
Gargoyle Magazine: "On The Eve Of Her Retirement, On A
Cross-Atlantic Flight, A United Airlines Stewardess
Picks Up The Microphone And Says Goodbye"
New Orleans Review: "Looking Out The Window Of The
Space Capsule," "Car Wreck Outside The Dinner
Party"

Affectionate thanks to family, friends and all ships at sea. To great pals Elisa Maranzana and Jack Jernigan; it's been a better party because you're here. Sisters and brothers back at the factory— Matthew Stevenson, Dean Paschal, Michael Stamm, Jennifer Levasseur, Kevin Rabalais, Lyn di Iorio, Jack Butler, Jim Bouton, Lewis Lapham and Louis van Gasteren—big heaps of gratitude and love. Finally, I'm deeply thankful to have had Russell Shorto's keen eye and ear during the writing of this book but even more grateful to have known his generosity and friendship—a dear friend on all continents. Dank je broer!

for Christa, Jesse Carter Christopher,
and Benjamin James

CONTENTS

ONE

TWO

THREE

Why couldn't we have seen this Old Nativity
while we were at it?
                              -- Elizabeth Bishop

Set the WABAC for the time of the Great Old Ones, Sherman.
Then go get that salt and rub it on your head.
                              -- Mister Peabody

ONE

On The Eve Of Her Retirement, On A Cross-Atlantic Flight, A United Airlines Stewardess Picks Up The Microphone And Says Goodbye

Should the urge arise
Porn stars should be permitted
To kiss when they fornicate.
I began feeling strongly about this—
And so much more—
About a million miles back
And should have spoken up.

Hold hands and determine
How we entered the world: Minor
Outlying islands? Small event of no
Great consequence? So many strangers
Snoring.
We do this, do that, and doggy-paddle.
We swim past the archipelagos we have
Invites for, beach up
On the Isle of Gilligan,
Or home.

Raise your hand if you can
Find your father's grave.
Uncanny isn't it?
We only had to flail naked
Under the moon
To get the numinous
Sea to grow inside us again.

I'm going to dim the cabin lights. Kiss whomever
You want. Welcome them back—
The Ancients, the Ocean, our
Dead Fathers—dozing up here near the bulkhead,
Against the wing.

Public Service Announcement
From Last Night's Dream

It's only a dream.
No one here turns into anyone else.
A mangled Confederate feeding
ice cubes to the grass
does not morph
into Senator Big Teeth crying
for a bendable straw
on the field of battle.

Here, county deputies prefer to tack
their deputy nags
between long rows of honeydew,
not corpses.

Here, an open compendium escapes
the Presidential Library; hides
in the men's room,
renders an affecting account
of The War
to Abe Lincoln at the urinal
and doesn't ask for an autograph.

In your every dream,
Harpo Marx will always be
Harpo Marx.
Not your mother.

It's clear as day.

We have here Berkeley Annie.
Remember her? She's forever perfecting
her personal religion of
Severe Casualness.
And why? Because 3 million
years ago she told a boy she was secretly
falling for (you)
Scram.

In the awake world she hikes the Berkeley
Hills, angling her sun hat
toward a sun that keeps setting
an hour ago,
hiding her hands
behind her like she's moving closer
toward a famous painting
or some tombstone. Or something.

She disappears. She comes back.
She disappears. She comes back.

If I have told you once,
I have told you a thousand times.

Car Wreck Outside The Dinner Party

In the end, it took only a horn blast to turn
the acreage over. Despair, the New Machinery—
all that stuff would no longer catch the ear.
We bad-vibed the plows into congregating
somewhere outside our view of the collision.
The dinner rolls left before the butter arrived
and then that general feeling of
free-floating general something
stepped inside.
We stared at the children.
What made us name them all Dylan?
Why so easily aggrieved, the wives of the Great
Authors?
"He's written more books than he's read you know
and he's only written two."
We went back to chewing the meat.
Can Juan get my hair to do that?
Did I just live the life of someone I don't know?
Look at us. Carefully setting the correct fork
next to the end of the world.

Hands

I like to hide
them behind me
like I'm sneaking up
on a Delacroix.
I like to point to the back row
when the tuba nails it;
sprinkle living daylight
to prime the inverse relationship
at the edge of the pit;
move my queen to Atom or Idea,
and just be done with it.

I like to tighten my cummerbund,
tip the tux;
hold the gold pan down deep
in the creek
'cause the square root of loss is pretty
much more of the same,
though the Penguin Hemisphere
keeps slipping through my fingers.

I like to hide a dime in a glove
and wave for mercy;
yet there's always a risk of taking
the fabric out too soon,
but that's the life of the hand for you.

After my friend's daughter
died he began building
one of those stone walls
you see all around New England.
This particular wall
only went shoulder high
because my friend could
never lift the heavy rocks
higher than his two grieving shoulders.

A mile of shoulder high wall
built by Suffering Man.
You see it everywhere.
Hushed, meandering line.
Border around everything left.
It took my friend forever
to build it, which, he said,
was fine by him.

Anger Writes Her First Love Letter
To Some Guy

I remember kissing you
Beneath The Awning Of The Silent Men.
I liked that you wanted me all to yourself.
You'd drop me, you'd picked me up.
Lose me, you'd turn back to find me.
Someone sees me, you'd hide me;
Someone hears me, you'd lie.
I was your quashed cry
Into a steering wheel, arc of water
Over tomatoes at dusk, firm grip into flesh
As the dryer-drum heated up the last dollar.
"O Anger," you'd say, "How I *love* me some Anger."
I was your rage running
Across the fairway toward the gale,
Giving lightning its chance to split
Open our skulls and light the way.
I followed you everywhere.
I was your last beer in the fridge.
Mozart's Requiem behind a Paywall.
And you my sweet,
You—warm bog turning up ancient tooth;
The little town Elvis fled.
The red corvette dying
One mile shy of the virgin's bed—
I'd be nothing without you.

Christmas Cards

Every year a few show up in our mailbox
addressed to some former occupants,
long gone.
Naturally, we open them up.
We forge the occasional check.
Admire the family pictures they send.
Then we make a place for them
next to legitimate cards on the mantel shelf
to face the most forgiving light
we can find in our room.

This year we admire the Spencers'
rescue dog named Fetch.
Father Spencer looks like he's whistling again,
which means trouble—he's hiding his fear
into another year.

And oh, how those boys have grown!
And that DeSoto smile, now bigger than ever
after a cancer scare almost collapsed the mortgage.

Didn't the McVies have a little baby?
What happened?

These are the times, fraught
with loss and doubt, to write letters
back to strangers in one's own blood:
Happy New Year, our alien sweethearts!

We love you too. Thank you for the Target Card!
WE LOVE YOU WE LOVE YOU WE LOVE YOU!
The kids have grown so tall!

The New Western Sky—Large, Seasonal Asterisms

That night, God said nothing
That added to our sadness.
Fallow fields, Great Gingivitis Outbreak Of '22,
Everything trailed us.

O large, seasonal asterisms—
Great Square of Pegasus, Diamond
Of Spring—blushing under your dot,
Welcome us, the wayward
Pilgrim to your slow train of wagon.

Agonic line,
Point us to the time
When the terror of discovering
New territory is as simple as saying,
Help yourself to everywhere I am.

Obliteration, High School Reunion

Smelling the ocean again, they were reminded of the ugly girl they went to high school with. Her real name had been flushed from their minds long ago but the resurrection of her queer malformation was easy work. It had jutted out below her lips like a fishing pier and they had called her *Rin-Chin-Chin* for it, right to her face, the cruelest of them, now in the wheelhouse of a beery load of middle-age memory driving down the night beach. The men zeroed in next on the high school homosexual—by far their softest mark—a black pixie boy in a pink cummerbund, a double-baton wizard whirl spinning fire preternaturally through his fingers as he marched our best through the center of town, right out in front where everyone would see him. What balls. Because in their hearts they knew the twirler knew everything about courage and the price it exacted, the men on the beach remained terrified of him, and not one went near to his given name, not even a sobriquet for him, save for the stock, 'faggot face,' or something near its dull, routine equal. Stopping the car to face the waves, the men gazed out in the dark, drinking and waiting for obliteration; warm in each other's company, but pining to be free from the nameless thing gaffing them each sorry evening. They droned on like an old sermon. They itemized their baton twirler's wild inferno of desire—twinkle toes, red nails, sequins, *heehee!* On and on it went into the night, the men parading it out, betraying their self-loathing and failure. Who among them possessed enough courage to say their state champ had never once dropped a baton he threw in the air? Never once caught on fire? Who among them knew the way to the twirler's peanut-butter-and-jelly-only-house, trophies floor to ceiling? The men had signed up for a ton of fun then promptly forgot to show up. And when they grew quiet, the sea and the sand and brilliant night sky, the music on the radio, it all swelled beneath their naked feet and said, *Put us back together.*

Village

That winter across the German border
'Learn To Laugh' lessons were free
and in our Dutch village
the canals froze
and we woke up dead too.

Outside the windows
our orphans ran, hurling
body onto hardness
like ice is the one thing
to carry anyone away
from whatever they begin the day
knowing they are.

We fought by linking arms
around big fires fueled
with the Oriental books
that massaged us too long
with how the world wasn't even real.
We sang,

go ahead big dogs,
attack the gate. We shall sweater
you and prop you on a toboggan and
point your open doggie faces toward
heaven where the gilded
rooster lives atop the church spire—
our last chicken twisting in the wind.

And when the cock crowed
once again,
Phantom villagers
who were never real
returned to sink deeply
in our laps—
their hands sweet
and begging us to forget them.

The Taormina Amphitheater

Perhaps I heard the confounding interest rate
slipping to Fuck You and a 1/2 Percent.
And maybe I sensed War was about to breakout
back home among the leaf blowers.
But I finally settled in, alone I hoped,
and got used to The Old Condition,
got to thinking about Kurosawa
pointing his camera at the sun
and how light is action
and Matriculate rhymes with Fate.
How the old gods liked to ignore
devotee spit fights, always slicing
Moon right down the middle
and telling Lee Marvin he has the
bigger half so no moon blood gets let.
I had travelled a long way
to a place that I had hoped would be empty.
Then out of nowhere, high up in the cavea,
Buzz Aldrin, God of Apollo, stood up
and punched some guy in the face
because the guy told Buzz the moon
he walked on was fake.
And when the God of Apollo
was leaving the amphitheater
he bent down and whispered to me,
"Nobody will believe you."

Kitty Carlisle, Actress, Raconteur, Tells Her Story To A Broken Record

Kit Carson once kicked me off his canoe.
We were filming, *"Tadpole, Absorb Your Tail And
Walk This Earth!"*
Nineteen synching lip. Four seasons
Of feather boa, another umpire late for the diamond.
I longed for the warm space in Kit's mitt;
Science, Applied *and* Pure.
How we flattered ourselves so imprecisely;
Like Senator Crunch-A-Bunch
Who could only fuck with his socks on.
We were weak dopes on the back
Lot. We let our men fall
In love with made up mountains,
Then cling wrap round the supper bone,
Rapid-eye-movement, sunny-side-down.
Hauling butt for the buttes
        whenever the dark cloud hit,
A man always needs some big price to pay.
One man leaves his home and never comes back.
Another man leaves his home and returns
with the milk.
We called the first one, The Blues.
The other one, Soul Train.
They gave me an Oscar for, *"I'm Talkin' Nonsense,
But You Get The Picture."*

Memorial Day

That afternoon, we watched a chicken-hawk
fly out of nowhere
to talon one of the white 'Peace Doves'
released from home plate
at the end of the Star Spangled Banner.
God it was funny.
Ten thousand of us, some nervously
laughing, shaded
our eyes from the bright, dying sun
that lights up the only rooms
we'll ever know.
We did the stadium wave.
Players cleared the benches.
Just the way we like it,
even the thing about the bird.
Halfway through the game
it all stopped. Rain.
We sat quietly
and waited for it all
to begin again, and I, for some reason
recalled a long, dark
night alone, the dishwasher
thumping out a rhythm
in the key of clean
while outside the house
it was pouring
and a storm was deadly
and a window broken.

But later on, there I was,
in the fourth inning
inside the Great Coliseum,
sensing everything was okay.
Maybe perfect.
The rain had stopped.
I looked way past where I was.
How long does it take for the tortoise
to cross the long trellis?
Oh, and how good the trout feels
in my hand after I've pulled it out
of the cold stream I keep trespassing.

Death On A Street

Look at us.
Old farts 'running' around
and around on an oval
of park dirt.
Laugh if you want. I do.
Every day I walk to the end
of my driveway, look
carefully both ways and cross
the street to get here.
Forgive me Myth.
Forgive me Holy;
you probably don't
deserve to be invoked
near this Action,
but on occasion
I've seen Nike unravel
and end up in knots.
I've seen Temple Dogs slobber
on golf balls that fall from God knows where.
And last night while sitting at the supper
table, my wife and I heard a harrowing
scream coming from the road. She
rushed ahead of me as I was saying
to her, *Breathe deep, Breathe,*
because I was afraid of what we'd find
out there.
It was bad.
A dog had been hit by a car.

The dog's owner, hysterical
and shaking, was kneeling in the middle
of the road over her brown Labrador.
The dog was conscious. The dog's tongue
was wagging and wet, but the breathing
labored. Neighbors kneeled down, one at a time,
to touch the terrified stranger, saying,
Things don't look too bad, sweetheart.
We said, Things will be okay.
And when the dog died
a few minutes later,
lying on a deep wound
the animal had hidden from us,
there was Dark Road. Quiet. Warmth.
And as far as wonders go,
it was really something.

*

TWO

Killers

For a long time,
You saw them everywhere.
One was a Zen monk
Without the Zen.
He killed light.
One was a child
Positioning a dead
Tooth under her pillow
For maximum shock effect.
The first book you read
After your mother was murdered
Was "In Cold Blood," by Truman Capote.
You would grow up
To be the kind that never confuses
John Hinckley with Mark David Chapman;
Jerry Lee Lewis with Lee Harvey Oswald.
You know your killers.
And one night, while reading
A paperback with your flashlight,
You looked into your young hand and
Saw yourself—in your own hand!—
Standing next to a road,
Pretending you were real.
It was snowing.
Maybe you were waiting for a bus.
You were waiting for something.
And everywhere, an indeterminate
glow.

A Selection From, *Best American Horse Thief Poems From The Loneliest Of Centuries, The 20th*

I left the horse near the mesa.
This one was a gossiper.
On and on about a
One-armed debutante back east.
I told the horse to shut up, to please shut up.
How many times did I tell him to shut up?
So I shot him.
Alone in the desert I count up
All the nights I drove
The blood donor mobile by your house.
You were French with a French accent.
Our love was an unfiltered UVB ray.
A friggin' C-5A.
I'd steal you an Appaloosa,
If I knew who you were.

My Bobcat Skid-Steer Loader
Is My Therapy

I was on top of it. Smoking cigars. Wow, was it hot. Maybe a hundred. I had just torn up a 30,000 sq. foot asphalt parking lot. Mikey boy, I say, you have kicked serious butt today. There was a party in my head. Then the manager steps out of the office. 'You demolished the wrong parking lot,' he says. Points at another high-rise hotel across the freeway and walks away. Damn! I say to myself, Why does this keep happening to me? I watch the manager back in his office, fiddling with the AC unit and making coffee. He was one cool dude, let me tell you. I mean, imagine not having a parking lot! I stayed up on the Bobcat all day and smoked and thought about things and smoked some more. At 5 o'clock, a helicopter lands in the rubble I made and the cool manager waves and ducks in. 'Have a nice evening,' he shouts, flying away. When it got dark I saw lights coming on in that hotel across the freeway. One at a time, here and there, rooms lit up. Every night the lights spell: OVER HERE OVER HERE

Looking Out The Window Of
The Space Capsule

We had cleared the towers,
Free to hate the rich again.
Big to-dos in the back forty;
Eighty-five days snockered
In the deep end, surfacing
Long enough to blame the maid
When the jewelry goes missing,
Hands down, best mechanic ever
Is rolling under my Firestones
As we speak,
That sort of crap.
Man, roger that.

O Terminus!
Out here in the blackness
You're not the end of the tether
But another shape contoured from our favorite stars,
The god of something way past
The god of envy, or perhaps the
Saint of Sheriffs In The Front Yard
Scribbling down everything
That had ever gone wrong. Or the
Heart surgeons confessing
The world they find
In our insides isn't
Particularly interesting,
And really, mostly water.

Work

They sat next to each other on the top step
of the porch beside the big trees
that grew near their house.
If the wind blew enough,
the trees would scratch
at the front windows.
The man pointed to a branch
bending over the house that clogged
the rain gutters. He touched the splintered
and bowed porch railing he wouldn't
lean against.
"This needs fixing too," the man said. "And
it's going to take a bunch of nails to do it."
"And paint too," the woman said.
The man fingered the white threads
curling at the end of the woman's cut-off jeans.
"The bottom step is all rotted out," she said.
"Not as bad as that one there," he said, pointing
away with his cigarette.
They talked some about cutting a hedge
and getting rid of some leaves but only
after they decided the grass had
faded and needed water.
The man squeezed the woman's hand
before he stood up.
"Not now," she told him.
And then the man sat back down and calculated
all the work to be done around him.

"What about the car?" he asked. "I forgot
about that."
"The car?"
"Doesn't it need a tune-up?"
"I don't think so," she said, slipping
her hand into his shirt pocket.
Then the man pulled soft hair from his wife's
face and gathered it tightly with both
hands. The woman dropped her head
between her knees and after she
lit her cigarette the man let
go and the wind took the
black hair and slapped it hard across
both their mouths.
And the branches clawed the house.
And the porch stung them with
crooked dry arms.
And the cigarettes
burned fast and blue, like factories
in their fingers, pouring
out an evening.

The Young Men At The Poetry Workshop Talk About Their Dead Fathers

You ever see that movie about those seven out-of-work samurai that get hired by these poor, miserable farmers to protect them and their depressing little village and then one day one of the young samurai is just fed up with it all, I mean super pissed, and he's really revved up and starts yelling at an old samurai about the nasty farmers and how they're thieves and low-rent and he's working himself into a big froth, and he likes that I think, I mean he's standing there with a sword in the rain about to bust a vein, and the old samurai looks kind of wise and lets him go on and on hoping he'll be spent soon I guess and the young, strong samurai is just heaving with rage and finally when he is almost out of breath he has to stop or he's going to drop dead and the old, wise samurai—he's sitting cross-legged in the dirt of course—the old samurai looks up into the face of the young samurai and says—you know, all kung-fu like— he goes, "You're a farmer's son, aren't you?" Oh man. I'd *love* to write a poem about that.

Inside A Zen Buddhist Temple,
An Intervention for Leonard Cohen

Listen,
the producer
whispered.

Lennie.
The new record.
Amazing!
A Masterpiece. Masterpiece!

Bad news is...
it's just not very
good.

Three Seconds Of Bright Light

She lines her body up under the sun
on a towel in her backyard and begins
thinking about the dead again.
First off is Austrian conductor Herbert von Karajan,
the impresario who piloted his own plane between
the two great orchestras he conducted—
rehearsing Mahler in Vienna, Beethoven
in Berlin—and she does her adding and taking away,
say 300 miles each way, maybe twice a week,
a little twin-engine jobber and she's calling
this lost hour in her high weeds, *Killing Time*.
As the white-headed maestro flies through her mind,
she pegs Karajan for the kind
of genius who maybe cut his own hair;
the sort of man who survived every shit-storm hurled
his way, sawing out a dining room table
from an oak he felled from his own forest
before flying to work to beg
a row of violins for something he called,
Three Seconds Of Bright Light, because for too long
said violins had put to slow ruination his beloved
Adagio
from Mahler Five.
Then she thinks,
where in this yard are the young men falling
for the sweet magnolia and rocky path?
Where is the friend spring cleaning an attic
or some stranger who has summered

too far away from the home he never should have left
and needs my understanding?
She eases up in the grass. She inches over to where
the sun has moved and subtracts the one sliver
of moonlight
that colored the one wall after that one night one week
when she put her hand through her bedroom window
just because the dog next door wouldn't stop barking
at the rain.

Thieves

Dear Eve:
Getting the fresh air like I was told
to, and more. Last night I went to a party
across the street, and everything was going
pretty swell I thought, but then the blue-gowned
hostess let loose of something like
"truth isn't the opposite of lying!"
and a room full of professors
went right to work on it,
trying to get to the bottom of things.

Eve, I followed along the best I could,
but I got lost.
I stared at the polished floor
and saw slick Italian shoes;
above me the still chandelier. The inside

voice said, *sneak out the back door and you
won't have to say goodnight to a single soul.*

I wasn't a thief
until the Sunday you crammed
all your stuff in the backseat
of our tired looking car,
and turned the corner—gone.
Now the best feeling is the heft
of Dr. Jenkins' gold Rolex
and Mrs. Langley's smooth boxes

of blank checks in the back
of a dark, desk drawer.

At this party a TV flickered in the corner.
On TV there was an old man hugging
onto a telephone pole
next to a floating Toyota.
And he was hugging hard, Eve,
like he'd been in all the Great Floods before,
and this time he wasn't letting go.
A helicopter hovered over him,
hunting for something left to save.
I looked at our house across the street.

The tiny porch light. The glow over the door.

Eve, I have robbed the neighborhood blind.
I squeeze through bathroom windows
on moonless nights, a cold thief.
I skip from house to house through wet grass,
a man in the world.
I fall asleep with a bucket
of shiny souvenirs next to my head.
And yet our neighbors return
to their front yards every morning,
doling out Wonder Bread
to the blue jays, sweeping
their front porches ten times a day.

What a queer bunch, Eve.
They wave over at me,
like nothing ever changes.

And when the old man on TV got plucked from
the flooded river with a rope the chopper
had guided over to him, it was the hostess
who raised her empty glass, singing,
Up up, and away!

Is this the way you remember things
in your old neighborhood, Eve?
The saved gliding over the treetops
with the sound turned off.
Hands pressed against a face,
holding on for sweet life.
The deep, deep dark in all the rooms,
in all the houses.

Supper At The Wake County Men's Shelter

I didn't know what a sonnet was
So I walked to the University
And googled it.
Here. Have one.
The book says loner always
Rhymes with boner.
This TV all plasma.
It's like kicking a seed up a glacier.
Tonight the poet will return.
He always comes back.
He always says he loves life
But really hates the world.
He'll put all this in a haiku.
And eat it.

Seeds

When she was my college roommate, Mother Teresa kept 'borrowing' my cigarette lighters. Once I say, "Hey Terry. You got enough of my lighters to burn down Calcutta!" (I think that put a seed in her brain.) Right away she copped an attitude and threw an ashtray at my head. Mother of God! I screamed. (I KNOW that put a seed in her brain!) But I chilled and tried to be Coolsville. After that Terry sort of wandered aimlessly around the apartment, day after day, wearing dark glasses, stooped over and depressed. Ashamed-like I would say, though she never said, I'm so ashamed, or, I'm so terribly sorry. Or anything. She cried a lot and quit eating and pretty much quit talking. Right in front of my eyes, my roomie turned into a sort of frail, little bird. One night while we were sitting on the couch watching TV, Terry let me hold her tiny head in my arms. I don't know why, but I began rocking her ever-so sweetly, you know, back and forth like she was my own little baby or something and I just said it, I whispered, "I forgive you. There. I love you and I forgive you." "Oh," she said softly, "so *that's* the way it's going to be."

Extempore, War

Germany has declared war on Russia—swimming in the afternoon.
Franz Kafka / August 2,1914, Journal Entry

Hemingway's only great book, that one about bull-
fighting.
He was such a dick to Sherwood Anderson.
The bastard!
Dragoons! Mounting flywheel!
Maps so sweetly expansive.
Oh well. Let's roll.
Our Republic promenades
right up to the build-up.
Cobblestone beveled means coup underfoot,
but no soul advancing.
We always bleat,
I'm so tired of the killing!! Tired of the killing!!
But we lie.
Two Generals at a table.
Small room, big fire.
One in living color.
The other hunts a peanut killed in the rug.
It's exactly like this, and photographs well.

Cigarettes

All night long twisting under the sheets,
then I just give up on sleep,
and go running instead.
A million times I've been up here,
jogging along the top of the levee
but not like this.
Some fog lifting off the Mississippi;
an empty stretch of marsh
where the herons usually stand;
things hadn't worked out
like we'd said they would
and she was back on a plane, heading home.
At the end
it was, *So tell me this Mr. Romeo—*
how come whenever I find
someone to love they never want to love me back?
Sprinting home I hear another kind of scream—
my father shouting into our bedrooms, Pray! Pray!
But his idea didn't work,
and she died anyway.
After that, he smoked his Winstons
at the edge of his bed—
sucking in smoke, his dead mother;
the boss whose guts he hated.
Everything left.

Soon the sun will rise
and the dark buildings

I'm running beside
will begin to brighten
and fill with workers like me,
where every day at noon
we shove aside our unfinished work
to squeeze out a narrow door
and cross the road together
so we can sit near the river
awhile and light cigarettes
and eat the food we've brought from home.
We'll walk a long way
just to gaze past the tall
white birds inching through the river;
our gold matches, one at a time,
spitting fire.

Grocery Store Under The Florida, Summer Sun

Uncouth to tell the dead
jogger she was half-way there.
Bracelet thingy
on the Pop-Tart shelf
begs to be tied up
with icing.
I love you, the boy says.
Fuck you, the girl says.
And if the magic mop
won't cool the floor
so spring the can and feel the cold pearl.
"O Baby. Let me hurt you."
And a delicious summer began its lie.

Kismet In The Eye Of The Camel

We read the proverbial Aramaic on the wall—Love me Forever! scratched into every wall in the cave. We ran out as fast as we could and lay next to a camel in the shade who seemed so much to adore us. "Your Beethoven," the camel asked my wife, "was he the deaf one or the blind one?" My wife closed her eyes (what eyes!) and lost herself to the camel's trance. "Skid marks on the road," she whispered. "Black at first. Seem to point to a certain place. Petering out just short of infinity." "Isn't that the Past?" the camel whispered. "It used to be the Past before it was Loss," she said. "Now it's Romance." "Ouh La La!!" the camel said. And my sweetheart wept. She snuggled against her camel and fell in love and saw all endings. "I feel like a moron," my wife sobbed. "There there," the camel said. "There there," I said. "I never meant for this to happen," the camel said. "I never mean for anything to happen."

Sorrow Is A Jet Plane In A Tiger Cage

Like you, my life
would have been different
if Mama Cass hadn't choked
on that chicken bone.
Man, you talk about wonder!
Monarch flutters a wing in Formosa then
Toto's house exploding in Kansas.
In First Class yonder, Paul (was he the fisherman?)
blows his nose and a fresh war in Timor.
You cash in a two dollar lottery ticket
and Grandma Moses goes into remission.
Down in the quadrants they recycle my mantra.
Forgiven parking tickets
sucked up in the cumulonimbus.
The first time she said, *sundry* I went
Coo-Coo for Cocoa Puffs
and shot a round into the aquarium.
Her autopsy of 'My Dead Guppy On The Carpet'—
"*Revealing*"
I phone ahead to the tiger at the zoo.
I promise to bring t-shirts in this language.

Please Allow Me To Introduce Myself.
I Am The Walrus. Your Hertz Rental

Jesse James & Arthur Rimbaud, pen-pals
you know, and Jesse heavy into haiku.

Know what else? Your father once
sat next to his buddy's casket in the hull
of a C-130 Transport all the way
from Saigon to Memphis, apologizing
to the dead soldier's mother
after the aircraft touched down, saying
he couldn't stay long,
needed back at the war
and besides, what he had to do was done.

I'm sorry your father couldn't
intimate to you how good he could be.

Did you know the only boss you ever loved
stabbed his second ex-wife in 1971?
And two lunar eclipses in 1600!
Wow. What a world.

The stars are lining up now,
as rental stars are wont to do,
telling me I'm to travel you
twenty straight hours across America
so you can learn what it is to be
a beat-up Confused About It All

dude in a desert motel.
Tonight, you're another traveling man
hoping to remember how Johnny Cash
once passed you on the river;
some cowboy, writing a
poem from the massif dust.

I Got To Thinking About The Old Stories

And looking around,
Seems like there's been some traveling done.
Haggard key.
A fridge won't smile.
Here's a ticket
To the ash I never left.
I'm certain there's soon to be an eclipse
Of something I'm about to get to.
That God isn't read
Like a dumbed-down thing
Is why we can't understand the sky.
How sad are the doctors
When they find our tumors?
Sometimes I look up
And see Blue, Apollo Blue.
But sometimes it's just
Dark, Weird, Galactica.

*

THREE

Valedictory For The World Weary Horsemen

Two wines once fed a multitude of broken fish.
John Wayne laments,
Women go to bed with John Wayne
But wake up with me.
What we hear coming round
The mountain could be the one we love
Singing, How Great Thou Art
To a sweet bubble of saffron.
Erect your own pantheon.
Then bomb it.
We are lightning-struck
And it makes no difference.
Our favorite oblate will score
A used humidor off eBay,
While America's first pregnant
Man becomes a preferred card holder.
Sunrise.
It's all ours.
Let's take it.
Today it looks like a sunburn
Punched itself in the face;
A violence of rainbow
Wreckage, unhitching the way.

Attention Shoppers: There's A Righteous Sunset Out In The Parking Lot And In Aisle 5, Two Anxious Virgins Whispered Softly To Each Other

There's a time and place for everything.
>Sean Connery for instance.

There's this new philosopher in Produce.
>God is the most obvious thing in the world.

I got the nun to confess that a quarter of a water
buffalo will only feed *one* Malawi village, *max*.
>I've always felt very connected to my body.

Sometimes I forget to eat.
>Will our hearts chew inside us
>when there's nobody to live it?

I keep forgetting to round up, once I minus you.
>I am afraid weeping men are slumped
>over the steering wheels.

Let's get out of here and never come out.
>Mortify the flesh to spook the tomato
>is how I register.

Yes! Flee the home and reek like hope!
>Cheekbones, rise to our occasion!

You feel like heaven to touch.
>I can't keep my ears off of you.

911

I got run over by the Whole Ball Of Wax.
Enlightened the inner ear.
My tongue cool
sleeping on the dog's breath,
while the good cross-eye
locked inward toward
the Guiding Light.
The sex parts tumbled
out the tumbler; hands smoothed
the wither of every jackass.
I saw the whole damn miracle!
Right here around my corner!
Yes, Wu Wei! Yes, Wabi-sabi!
Yes, Shortbread Cake and Channel 4!
Okay. I lie.
It was just so hot.
My feet were tired.
My shoes were tired of my feet.
I was tired of my shoes.
My tired was tired of me.
So I stopped.
I stopped in the road and lay down
and took a long nap.
And I'm not sure
if I'm awake.

Christmas Dinner, Brooklyn

He was drunk and frightened,
Spitting his last lump of dead lung
Into a red reindeer napkin
And then hiding it between
His knees, but knowing
The whole family had seen it.

A silent night fogged in over the peas.
Everyone reached for their wine,
On the count of one.

We began to talk—
Musket and magi
At controlled room temp
Next to cool Rothko....
Lame haircuts splitting
Rent and cable...

And then the dying man
Straightened up one last time.
"Walt Whitman," he said.
"My man lived in a tiny house
In Camden, you know. A brick
Out front with *WW*
Burned into it.
And now there's a prison!
Right across the goddamn street!
And not a very nice one either."

The Morning After My Toddler Shat
In The Shallow End

We were welcomed back.
A sleepy looking paladin,
the first to climb the guard tower,
told us that Paul Newman also
drank a case of Budweiser a day
and that he sank that enviable face
into a bucket of ice each morning,
so the chorister sang from the pool,
     To Begin Again.

And so we did.

Between the ropes a clarinet dove,
chancing in the blind spots
and the porous distance called.

The women began the day
under the Parasol of Diminishing Hope,
barraging their offspring with High-Five
Awesomes! as the little dummies
bobbed from the shallow.

The sun grew warm
and sent us a wake of jam.

It would be autumn soon
and we'd be somewhere else.

We'd be reading to the blind every
other Saturday, and oh...
the little, winter fibs
to be told to the loved ones.

But now, the groins ached
with the arc of every woman's back
while the absurdly expensive
crepe myrtles watched
our final days
in the replenished pool.

Looking Out My Hospital Window, W/ December 9

I wasn't much for the star.
I was a beach guy; before
That, I'm all mountain.
But I do love me some moon.

And here I am at the end.
Not a hall or a book or the soup,
But me!
The end of me!

Looking back,
It's cool my ancestors invented
Things like Self-Awareness and Foreplay.
And to think after all this time
I never met anyone born on March Twenty-Nine!
And somewhere down in the parking lot there's
A certain June Two, picking up the asphalt glint
In her eye and I have to admit
I'm happy she's miserable
Knowing I'm here alone, flat on my back
Saying bye-bye to our sky.

Chalk it up as, *Successful Life*;
Hey. I was loved!
And remember this: 'Funeral' is not Latin for 'Fun.'
Don't, *Let us celebrate his life*—when I'm done.
Ball your eyes out! I'm dead!

Because take it from me—
If you don't miss the dead,
You'll never get rid of them.

I remember after September 11th,
The Queen of England spoke at our National
Cathedral, saying just eight words:
"Grief is the price you pay for love."

Look at those stars!
December 9, come draw my blood!
My heart? Here, take it!
It's about to burst with love.

That other heart, sort of small
And black and cold,
You'll find it cowering behind my rib
Clutching its own calendar,
Fretting about DEATH.
Just ignore that heart.
That's what I did.
Well...tried.

Dressage In Its Sea Of Reincarnation

If tomorrow we are the widow
Curtseying to the bottom of the sea,
Or say the indigent sailor holding up the old shell
To the dark, can we still be a black knife
Falling into a toaster?
Ancient amoeba capsized?
Will the abandoned ship return
To its Dancing Horse?
Now the coo-coo tock is ticking
Off one thing it can count on—

> *Two old brothers and their wives*
> *Trespassing onto a private beach*
> *On New Year's Day.*
>
> *Windy and cold,*
> *the old women help the old men*
> *Out of their clothes,*
> *Coats and shoes and trousers and shirts,*
> *Underwear, everything, a pile in the sand.*
>
> *Then the brothers held hands,*
> *And ran, and dove under our surf, just to*
> *Surface and howl and return through this*
> *Backwash.*

It Was A Bad Time To Be Named Henry Kissinger

For years I received letters stinking
of jungle rot: Dear Poisonous Frog,
Dear Two-Headed Snake, do you know
the hell you've wrought?
But let's be honest.
It was a coup for me
Henry, and I'm grateful.
Sharing your ignoble name
gave me the excuse I needed
not to answer my telephone
for decades.
Things as they were then—kids
leaving home without a word, why?
Yippies, no postcard....no nothing,
I was terrified I might receive
a call from the lost son I loved
and have to return some, I love you
when it was time to hang up.
What sad toads we were Henry.
Still, I was only Henry Kissinger,
Teaneck, New Jersey.
Henry pulling weeds.
Henry watching a phone tremble.
My neighbors know me.
They can tell you everything.

New Year's Day Redemption

The autumn your daddy died
you hid under the high school stadium
to sucker punch every boy you loved.

On the last dawn of this year,
you tie up your bathrobe
and shout, Fuck Redemption!
you old, bloated word taking up my couch!

You climb to the roof of your house
to curse the nihilists aiming
high-grade fireworks
at anything that looks alive.

What a year!
Confessing to the joy of pummeling
the hell out of someone
to make certain there was nothing
left remaining of them to lose.

You've taught yourself
how to straddle a chimney.
Taught yourself how to pull
your neighbors close to you.
Oh, to sit on a house and roll weed
and get all supernatural under the night!

Are those your children
entering the garden
below your body?
Lighting sparklers?
Listen. They're counting backwards
toward the one second
that never sleeps—
Straight up, transcendent
midnight—the
second that isn't today anymore
or tomorrow either.

Moveable Feast

That's what we had christened our minivan.
But soon the children were brown and chiseled
Surfing Serbian pipeline, Hinterland.
The engine groaned in the yard
And we began to call it, FORD.
In the evenings we pressed our faces in the dirt
To hear a musket snuggle under okra.
Acre of broom straw
Your hair fine enough to sleep in!
All in all, still a Glory Farm.
Dolly Parton, your bust so enormous
Because your heart, you say, so filled,
So gigantic and so pure, bursts all
Wonder to a fore,
Help us unbutton the Last Scroll!
A mouse shivers above Food Lion.
Amazing Grace is trapped
In a speaker and the new fathers
Are walking out of the sun
To eat beneath it.

Incidental, Stoic Morning

If I were a stinky sponge left to dry alone
  over the catch drain
I'd go, "At least I'm not a Saturday night in 1974."
That singer from Radiohead sounds a whole lot like
  the singer from Bread.
My angel is a big, bad wash of white wing.
  Dervish Whirl around the cheese wheel.
I notify the Curia
  that love survived their night.
I line-out the old libretto
  below the fold; buzz the river
With the copter and now know
  where all the old pay phones go.
I've put fencing back on the table
  and nuclear options think
I'm making my way now, meaning,
  I wish I would have shared the plum.

A dozen times a morning,
  I touch my son's face.
I do rights on red.
  The stove does fire.
A woman
  breaks the egg.

Little Walter Returns From The Dead To Deliver A Mournful, Seaside Elegy At Blues Harmonica Camp

Jesus donkey riding girly-style
through his adoring crowd of Killers.
Two beats later curled up
like a cosmonaut
slobbering hungry
for the New Way Out.
That, my friends, we call
Glissando.

Refinanced double-wides balanced
atop Saturn Boosters are nothing
but a reminder that thoughtful arrangements
of plastic chairs inside the home are crucial
in reflecting, New World View.

James Cotton's tongue blocks.
Howlin' Wolf's fingers in the dark.
Used to be you could hear the long-haired
women scissor-kicking beneath the Atlantic
if you were quiet enough
but that's probably gone too.

When my baby brother died
I said Good-bye World
and went to live under a tree.
Un-talent yourselves.

Mourn the satellites that
orbit and burn and fall.

This ocean pier will forever hold
our unborn daughters
and their unborn fishing rods
and all of our mothers,
singing.

Out At Sea

Let's go get some fish.
We can catch more than we need.
We can roam around and get lost.
Maybe we'll care about being lost
And maybe we won't.
And if we're far out at sea,
And brother we are,
Let's eat all we catch!
Aboard this boat we'll say
Something nice
About the fish before we gut them.
After all, they're lovely fish
And not the place we come from.
Let us drop bait into every corner
Of every ocean that will have us.
Yes, there is great abundance
And only a few things terrible.

Sleep Tablet

I have a dream.
I have a dream that The Great Fire of Money
Won't touch our toes
And that The Church promises
To stop raping our children.

I have a dream that a calendar
Filled with Civil War meet-ups
Is History quitting the Past
And a Holy Galore of collectible
Choo-choos is just Her Majesty
Waving to a brick.

My dream is that the hounds
Will be the first to give up
Their grief and not a snivel about last season's
Defense because God's light remains
Translucent and every dog gets this.

I dream that the Prophets
Continue to bleed into our lumber
And the winters are short
And the doorbells ring.

I have a dream we're a temporary thing.
A temporary thing whirling
beneath one Ancient Paddle Wheel,
The din of dawn encroaching;

The fan never falling, and the drip,
Drip, drip of water on this rock.

Extended Remarks
At The Awards Banquet

To my boyhood friend Muzzy Crumpler who
wanted to be Bob Dylan and fashioned
a harmonica holder out of a coat
hanger but only succeeded in hanging
himself with it, I love you brother.

Here's to Ayn Rand at the soup kitchen
because our 51st state, the great state
of Common Sense, sentenced her
to 55 bazillion hours of community service
for being just plain nasty. Kiss my ass Ayn Rand!

Before Barbara Streisand thanks
all the Little People again
I want to say something
to the guy who wakes up every day
feeling like a rug bunched under the chair wheel,
the guy who buys a shaver with 64 blades
and a hundred-volt battery and wonders
how his face caught fire.
Brothers, keep waving in case
your ex-children walk by;
Keep the fanny Cha-Cha-Cha-ing.

Here's to an insecure God,
because no matter how often
we thank him for his Mercy

we feel compelled to add,
Really. We're Serious.

Friends. Every day a stranger lifts a Toyota off our
legs.
    Our building is always burning;
      A rapier is wrested from the heart
And the ATM spits out another mill
      When we only need a tad.

    And each night when we cross the desert
      We are alone with a dragon and
        Lord, how your stars are abundant
         with no apparent design.

Michael Martin's poetry has been published in many literary journals including *New Orleans Review, Carolina Quarterly, Berkeley Poetry Review*, and *Chattahoochee Review*. He co-founded the literary magazine, *Hogtown Creek Review*, and for many years he was a feature writer for *Amsterdam Weekly*. He has edited numerous magazines and books, including *Rules Of The Game: The Best Sports Writing From Harper's Magazine*.

Extended Remark: Poems From A Moravian Parking Lot is his first collection of poetry. He lives in Raleigh, North Carolina with his wife and two boys.

To contact the author, e-mail: mmartin600@gmail.com

Made in the USA
San Bernardino, CA
10 March 2015